How to Start a Home Based Travel Agency Workbook

By
Tom and Joanie Ogg CTC MCC

Published by

Tom Ogg & Associates

P.O. Box 2398
Valley Center, California 82082
1-760-751-1007
TomOgg@aol.com
http://www.HomeBasedTravelAgent.com

ISBN# 978-1484162088
10 9 8 7 6 5 4 3 2 1

Because laws and interpretations change, and
because a written sentence, or paragraph may be
subject to different interpretations, this book
is sold with the specific understanding that the authors
are neither members of the bar in any state, nor licensed
CPAs and are not offering or rendering legal or accounting
advice. Any reference made to those topics within the
book should be addressed to members of those
professions hired as such.

The authors do not assume, and hereby disclaim any
liability to any party for all loss and damage caused by
errors and omissions in "**How to Start a Home-Based Travel
Agency Workbook**" whether such errors and omissions
result from negligence, accident or any other cause. While
every effort has been made to complete the most current
information available at press time, the authors urge
readers to consult specialists for up-to-the-minute
information regarding any topic in this book.

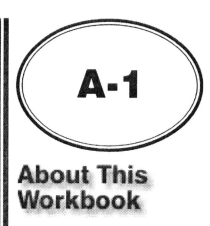

About This Workbook

This workbook is designed to help you gain an understanding of the task of starting your own home-based travel business. There are many subtle ideas one must understand in order to make the right decisions and reduce the amount of wasted time and effort. It is printed on only one side of a page leaving plenty of room for notes and other information gathering. Since it is your own private study guide, you can use it on an ongoing basis to refer to your thoughts and ideas as you progress. It is divided into three sections.

The workbook questions are broken into conceptual modules that coincide with chapters of the text. They are designed as a tool for you to examine the elements introduced in the text with which you will need to become familiar. The questions are open-ended and allow you to explore your thinking about your specific business.

The Start-up Checklist is designed so that you can estimate the cost and prioritize your time during the start-up process.

Finally, at the end of the workbook is a test. You can take the test to see how well you have comprehended the information presented in the study course and workbook. If there are questions that you do not know the answers to, you can always go back to the study

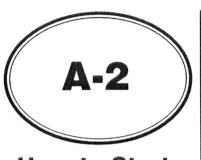

How to Start a Home Based Travel Agency Workbook

course and uncover them.

Enjoy the process of learning about starting and operating a home-based travel agency and I wish you all the luck in the world. I will look forward to seeing you one day on a cruise seminar or other travel forum.

Tom Ogg

Module One
Historical Overview

Workbook Exercises 1-5

To Accompany
Text Chapters 1 -3

By completing this module you will:

• *Gain a historical perspective of the travel industry.*

• *Understand the evolutionary process from storefront to home-based agencies.*

• *Identify the factors that contributed to this transition.*

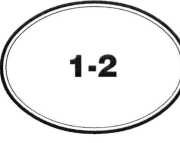

1-2

How to Start a
Home Based
Travel Agency
Workbook

Notes

1. What are some of the main reasons that this is a perfect time to consider a career as a travel entrepreneur?

_____

_____

_____

_____

_____

_____

_____

_____

_____

_____

_____

_____

_____

_____

2. What is the "CRS"? Detail its evolution to the present state?

_____

_____

_____

_____

_____

_____

_____

_____

_____

_____

_____

_____

**Module One
Historical
Overview**

1-3

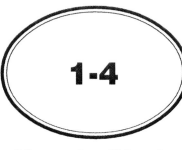

1-4

How to Start a Home Based Travel Agency Workbook

Notes

3. What changes/events occurred in the industry to create the move from large storefront agencies to the new home-based model?

_____

_____

_____

_____

_____

_____

_____

_____

_____

_____

_____

_____

_____

_____

_____

4. What are three factors that influence a retail agency's ability to make a profit? Explain how these factors work together to measure productivity?

_____

_____

_____

_____

_____

_____

_____

_____

_____

_____

_____

_____

_____

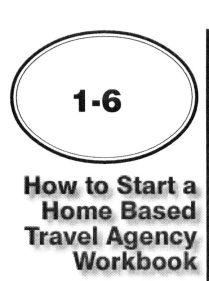

1-6

How to Start a Home Based Travel Agency Workbook

Notes

_____
_____
_____
_____
_____
_____
_____
_____
_____
_____
_____
_____
_____
_____
_____
_____
_____
_____
_____
_____
_____
_____
_____
_____
_____
_____
_____
_____
_____
_____
_____
_____
_____
_____
_____
_____
_____
_____
_____
_____

3. Specifically, how has airline deregulation affected the travel industry? Examine its impact from both the airlines and travel agency communities' perspective.

_____
_____
_____
_____
_____
_____
_____
_____
_____
_____
_____
_____
_____
_____
_____
_____
_____
_____
_____
_____
_____
_____
_____
_____
_____
_____
_____
_____
_____

1-7

**Module One
Historical
Overview**

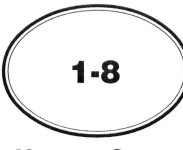

1-8

**How to Start a
Home Based
Travel Agency
Workbook**

Notes

Module Two
The Independent
Contractor

Workbook Exercises 6 -12

To Accompany
Text Chapter 4

By completing this module you will:

• *Understand the differences between an Independent Contractor and an Outside Sales Person.*

• *Identify the specific criteria the IRS uses to determine this classification.*

• *Assess the "pros" and "cons" of both designations.*

2-2

How to Start a
Home Based
Travel Agency
Workbook

Notes

_____
_____
_____
_____
_____
_____
_____
_____
_____
_____
_____
_____
_____
_____
_____
_____
_____
_____
_____
_____
_____
_____
_____
_____
_____
_____
_____
_____
_____
_____
_____
_____
_____
_____
_____
_____
_____
_____

6. Why is it important to make a distinction between your status as an "outside-sales employee" or a "true independent contractor" (both for the agent and agency)?

_____

_____

_____

_____

_____

_____

_____

_____

_____

_____

_____

_____

_____

_____

7. List at least six (6) of the rules the IRS considers when determining your classification and how they affect you.

_____

_____

_____

_____

_____

_____

_____

_____

_____

_____

_____

_____

_____

_____

2-3

**Module Two
The
Independent
Contractor**

2-4

**How to Start a
Home Based
Travel Agency
Workbook**

Notes

8. State at least two (2) reasons why an employee is better than an independent contractor for the agency.

_____
_____
_____
_____
_____
_____
_____
_____
_____
_____
_____
_____
_____
_____
_____
_____

9. State at least two (2) reasons why an independent contractor is better than an employee for the agency.

_____
_____
_____
_____
_____
_____
_____
_____
_____
_____
_____
_____
_____
_____

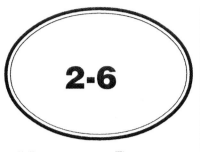

2-6

How to Start a
Home Based
Travel Agency
Workbook

10. Now, state at least two (2) reasons why being an employee is better than an independent contractor from the agent's perspective.

_____
_____
_____
_____
_____
_____
_____
_____
_____
_____
_____
_____
_____

11. Finally, state at least two (2) reasons why being an independent contractor is more advantageous than being an employee.

_____
_____
_____
_____
_____
_____
_____
_____
_____
_____
_____
_____
_____
_____

2-7

**Module Two
The
Independent
Contractor**

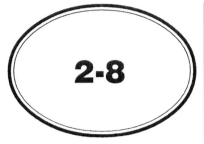

2-8

How to Start a
Home Based
Travel Agency
Workbook

Notes

12. Having had a chance to consider all the "pros and cons", which role fits you best and why?

_____
_____
_____
_____
_____
_____
_____
_____
_____
_____
_____
_____
_____
_____
_____
_____
_____
_____
_____
_____
_____
_____
_____
_____
_____
_____
_____

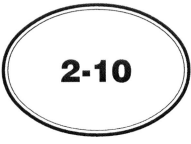

2-10

How to Start a
Home Based
Travel Agency
Workbook

Notes

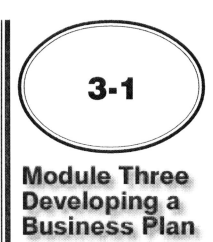

**Module Three
Developing a
Business Plan**

Workbook Exercises 13-16

**To Accompany
Text Chapters 5 & 6**

By completing this module you will:

•*Recognize the value of creating a business concept and business plan.*

•*Identify the components of the travel entrepreneur's business plan.*

•*Develop a business concept.*

•*Explore your business expectations.*

•*Establish your business goals and create a business plan.*

3-2

**How to Start a
Home Based
Travel Agency
Workbook**

Notes

13. What are overrides?

_____
_____
_____
_____
_____
_____
_____
_____
_____
_____
_____
_____
_____
_____
_____

14. You have been provided with some basic information on the traditional yields for the various products one might sell. In an attempt to keep you "focused", which product(s) interest you? Which would you find the most rewarding to sell?

_____
_____
_____
_____
_____
_____
_____
_____
_____
_____
_____
_____
_____

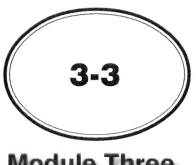

3-3

**Module Three
Developing a
Business Plan**

3-4

How to Start a
Home Based
Travel Agency
Workbook

Notes

15a. If specialization is the name of the game, after reading the "15 Areas of Opportunity to Make Lots of Money" which best fits your entrepreneurial vision? Or perhaps you have considered an area of specialization not mentioned. As you begin to "focus" on your new business venture, identify the market you plan to pursue and state why you believe that is a viable direction for you to follow.

_____

_____

_____

_____

_____

_____

_____

_____

_____

_____

_____

_____

15b. Assess the knowledge you possess to establish your niche.and the knowledge that you need to obtain.

_____

_____

_____

_____

_____

_____

_____

_____

_____

_____

_____

_____

_____

_____

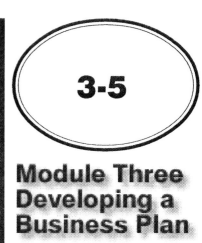

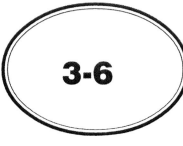

3-6

**How to Start a
Home Based
Travel Agency
Workbook**

Notes

16. Remember, <u>How to Start a Home Based Travel Agency</u> is an action oriented text. Therefore, in the space provided, outline your basic business plan.

a). Define your expectations (include both short and long term goals:

_____
_____
_____ \
_____
_____
_____

b). State your specific objectives:

_____
_____
_____ \
_____
_____
_____

c). Project your income:

_____
_____
_____ \
_____
_____
_____

d). Project your expenses:

_____
_____
_____ \
_____
_____
_____

e). How do plan to fund your new business?

_____
_____
_____

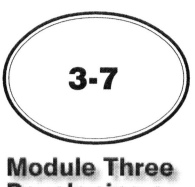

3-7

**Module Three
Developing a
Business Plan**

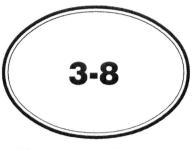

3-8

How to Start a
Home Based
Travel Agency
Workbook

Notes

Module Four
Establishing
Your Business

Workbook Exercises 17-21

**To Accompany
Text Chapter 7**

By completing this module you will:

•*Become aware of the steps necessary to launch your business.*

•*Take action to organize your travel business.*

•*Assess your options and needs in order to establish an environment conducive for operating a home-based business.*

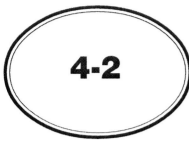

4-2

How to Start a
Home Based
Travel Agency
Workbook

Notes

17. What steps must you take to establish your business name?

_____
_____
_____
_____
_____
_____
_____
_____
_____
_____
_____
_____
_____
_____
_____
_____

18. Name three (3) different ways you can organize (operate) your business and state one advantage to each.

_____
_____
_____
_____
_____
_____
_____
_____
_____
_____
_____
_____
_____
_____
_____
_____

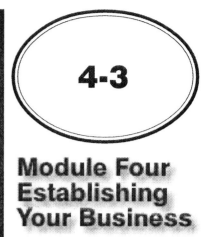

4-3

**Module Four
Establishing
Your Business**

4-4

How to Start a
Home Based
Travel Agency
Workbook

Notes

19. What is a "Client Security Trust Account" and why is it important?

_____

_____

_____

_____

_____

_____

_____

_____

_____

_____

_____

_____

_____

_____

20. Why is it important to establish an exclusive space for your "home-office"?

_____

_____

_____

_____

_____

_____

_____

_____

_____

_____

_____

_____

_____

_____

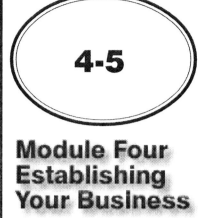

4-5

**Module Four
Establishing
Your Business**

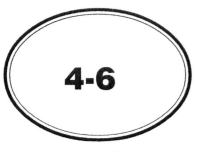

4-6

**How to Start a
Home Based
Travel Agency
Workbook**

Notes

21. In order to establish a productive work space, what are the minimum requirements in terms of office furniture, equipment and supplies?

_____

_____

_____

_____

_____

_____

_____

_____

_____

_____

_____

_____

_____

_____

_____

_____

_____

_____

_____

_____

_____

_____

_____

_____

_____

_____

_____

_____

4-7

**Module Four
Establishing
Your Business**

4-8

How to Start a
Home Based
Travel Agency
Workbook

Notes

Module Five Operating a Home Based Business

Workbook Exercises 22-28

To Accompany
Text Chapters 8 - 9

By completing this module you will:

•*Examine your sources of revenue and expenses.*

•*Apply this knowledge to organize your books and manage your finances.*

•*Modify your home environment to establish a successful base of operations for your business.*

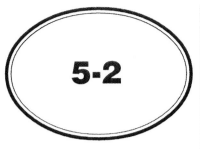

5-2

How to Start a Home Based Travel Agency Workbook

Notes

22. Based on your business plan, what do you anticipate as being your main sources of revenue?

_____
_____
_____
_____
_____
_____
_____
_____
_____
_____
_____
_____
_____
_____
_____
_____

23. Having identified your anticipated revenue sources, develop a prototype of an account chart to manage your bookkeeping needs.

_____
_____
_____
_____
_____
_____
_____
_____
_____
_____
_____
_____
_____
_____

5-4

How to Start a
Home Based
Travel Agency
Workbook

Notes

24. Now let's take a look at your expenses. Below are a list of expenses you will most likely incur, identify under what expense account entry they should be itemized.

a). Your business cards:

_____
_____
_____
_____
_____

b). This manual and related text materials:

_____
_____
_____
_____
_____

c). Services such as your DSL or Internet access provider:

_____
_____
_____
_____
_____

d). Paying your tax advisor:

_____
_____
_____
_____
_____

e).Taking your client to lunch:

_____
_____
_____
_____
_____
_____
_____

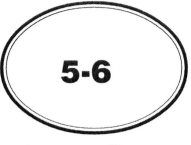

5-6

How to Start a
Home Based
Travel Agency
Workbook

Notes

25. If you plan to expense your automobile, what documentation is required by the IRS?

_____

_____

_____

_____

_____

_____

_____

_____

_____

_____

_____

_____

26. In a home-based business, maintaining the separation of your personal and professional life is mandatory, but difficult. Identify five (5) strategies or ideas you plan to implement to address this challenge (Be specific as to how you will enforce your plan).

_____

_____

_____

_____

_____

_____

_____

_____

_____

_____

_____

_____

_____

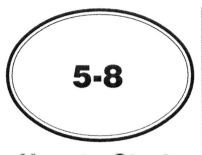

5-8

**How to Start a
Home Based
Travel Agency
Workbook**

Notes

27. You have made a decision that meeting clients in your home is not an option. List five (5) alternative locations that you can use to conduct business.

_____
_____
_____
_____
_____
_____
_____
_____
_____
_____
_____
_____
_____
_____

28. As a home-based entrepreneur, list five (5) steps you can take to assure your business credibility and promote a professional image.

_____
_____
_____
_____
_____
_____
_____
_____
_____
_____
_____
_____
_____
_____
_____

5-10

How to Start a
Home Based
Travel Agency
Workbook

Notes

Module Six
Computer Basics

Workbook Exercises 29-34

**To Accompany
Text Chapter 10**

By completing this module you will:

•*Identify the computer hardware components and software applications needed to effectively conduct your home-based business.*

•*Assess your computer needs based on your business plan.*

•*Select the proper computer equipment to accomplish your goals.*

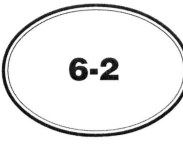

6-2

How to Start a Home Based Travel Agency Workbook

Notes

_____
_____
_____
_____
_____
_____
_____
_____
_____
_____
_____
_____
_____
_____
_____
_____
_____
_____
_____
_____
_____
_____
_____
_____
_____
_____
_____
_____
_____
_____
_____
_____
_____
_____
_____
_____
_____

29. What is the most important reason that a notebook computer is preferable to a desktop when it comes to your home-based business enterprise?

_____
_____
_____
_____
_____
_____
_____
_____
_____
_____
_____
_____
_____

30. What is a CPU? Explain its function or purpose.

_____
_____
_____
_____
_____
_____
_____
_____
_____
_____
_____
_____
_____
_____
_____
_____

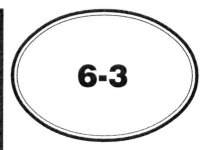

6-4

How to Start a Home Based Travel Agency Workbook

31. If your computer budget is extremely limited, what would be the minimum operating speed you should consider?

_____

_____

_____

_____

_____

_____

_____

_____

_____

_____

_____

_____

_____

_____

_____

32. What is the significance or value of a CD-RW/DVD disk drive?

_____

_____

_____

_____

_____

_____

_____

_____

_____

_____

_____

_____

_____

_____

_____

_____

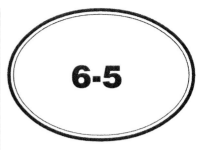

6-5

**Module Six
Computer
Basics**

6-6

How to Start a Home Based Travel Agency Workbook

Notes

33. Let's talk computer components. You have identified your needs and are armed and ready to purchase your computer. What are you prepared to tell the salesman you want and how you intend to use it? Consider each of these primary components as it relates to your needs:

a). Processor

_____
_____
_____
_____

b). RAM

_____
_____
_____

c). Hard Drive

_____
_____
_____

d). Disk, Jump and CD/DVD Drives

_____
_____
_____
_____

e). Monitor

_____
_____
_____

f). Printer

_____
_____
_____
_____
_____

6-8

How to Start a
Home Based
Travel Agency
Workbook

Notes

34. Now let's look at the software you intend to use. What marketing and operational software do you deem absolutely mandatory for the success of your business? Prioritize them in order of importance to you and your anticipated success.

_____
_____
_____
_____
_____
_____
_____
_____
_____
_____
_____
_____
_____
_____
_____
_____
_____
_____
_____
_____
_____
_____
_____
_____
_____
_____
_____
_____
_____

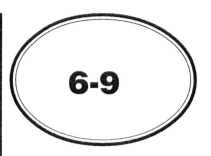

**Module Six
Computer
Basics**

6-10

How to Start a Home Based Travel Agency Workbook

Notes

Module Seven
Developing a Host Agency Relationship

Workbook Exercises 35-43

To Accompany
Text Chapter 11

By completing this module you will:

• *Examine the dynamics of the host agency/independent contractor relationship.*

• *Predict your needs within the parameters of this relationship.*

• *Understand the importance of a written contract and the essential elements that must be addressed.*

• *Prepare a selection process for establishing this relationship.*

7-2

How to Start a
Home Based
Travel Agency
Workbook

Notes

35. Why are offers such as, "Become a Travel Agent for $495" considered shams?

_____
_____
_____
_____
_____
_____
_____
_____
_____
_____
_____
_____
_____

36. When it comes to commission splits, let's say you sold a cruise for $3000. Would it be more lucrative to work with an agency that offers you 80% of a 10% commission or one that offers 50% of an 18% commission? Explain your answer.

_____
_____
_____
_____
_____
_____
_____
_____
_____
_____
_____
_____
_____
_____

7-4

How to Start a
Home Based
Travel Agency
Workbook

Notes

37. Why is the geographical location of your host agency an important consideration?

_____

_____

_____

_____

_____

_____

_____

_____

_____

_____

_____

_____

_____

_____

38. Based on the key considerations for negotiating an agreement with a host agency delineated in this book, list the issues on a continuum, from most to least important to you.

_____

_____

_____

_____

_____

_____

_____

_____

_____

_____

_____

_____

_____

7-6

How to Start a Home Based Travel Agency Workbook

Notes

39. Now, look at the top three issues most important to you for establishing your host agency agreement. State reasons why you have placed such high priority on these specific considerations.

_____
_____
_____
_____
_____
_____
_____
_____
_____
_____
_____
_____
_____

40. As an independent contractor, it is time to enter into a formal written agreement. What is indemnification and why is it an important aspect of the agreement?

_____
_____
_____
_____
_____
_____
_____
_____
_____
_____
_____
_____
_____
_____

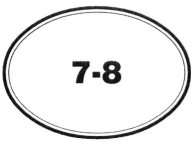

7-8

**How to Start a
Home Based
Travel Agency
Workbook**

Notes

41. As an independent contractor, what IRS form must be used to report your income?

_____

_____

_____

_____

_____

_____

_____

_____

_____

_____

_____

_____

_____

_____

42. Explain the importance of the "ownership of accounts" clause?

_____

_____

_____

_____

_____

_____

_____

_____

_____

_____

_____

_____

_____

_____

_____

_____

_____

_____

_____

7-10

**How to Start a
Home Based
Travel Agency
Workbook**

Notes

43. What would be the risks involved in not establishing a formal written contract with a host agency or independent contract network?

_____

_____

_____

_____

_____

_____

_____

_____

_____

_____

_____

_____

_____

_____

_____

_____

_____

_____

_____

_____

_____

_____

_____

_____

_____

_____

_____

_____

7-11

**Module Seven
Developing a
Host Agency
Relationship**

7-12

How to Start a Home Based Travel Agency Workbook

Notes

Module Eight
Working with Suppliers and Reservations Systems

Workbook Exercises 44-49

**To Accompany
Text Chapter 12 & First-half of Chapter 13
(13-1 to 13-6)**

By completing this module you will:

• *Discover the industry credentials and requirements for working with suppliers.*

• *Create a plan for validating yourself as a travel professional with suppliers.*

• *Compare the reservation systems available to travel agents.*

• *Formulate a way utilize the multitude of reservation systems to your advantage.*

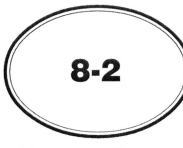

8-2

How to Start a Home Based Travel Agency Workbook

Notes

44. What is the difference between a Travel Agent Identification Number and a Pseudo Identification Number?

_____
_____
_____
_____
_____
_____
_____
_____
_____
_____
_____
_____
_____
_____
_____

45. There are basically four channels to embrace in obtaining a Travel Agent ID Number (not a Pseudo ID Number). What are they and what requirements must be met to obtain each?

_____
_____
_____
_____
_____
_____
_____
_____
_____
_____
_____
_____
_____
_____
_____

8-4

How to Start a Home Based Travel Agency Workbook

Notes

46. What if you do not meet the qualifications to obtain a Travel Agent ID Number? What options can you pursue in order to sell travel and receive commission?

_____
_____
_____
_____
_____
_____
_____
_____
_____
_____
_____
_____
_____

47. There are four major automated travel agency systems used in the United States. Name these CRS/GDS vendors.

_____
_____
_____
_____
_____
_____
_____
_____
_____
_____
_____
_____
_____
_____
_____
_____

8-6

How to Start a Home Based Travel Agency Workbook

Notes

48. Is it absolutely necessary for a travel agent to have access to a CRS/GDS system in order to sell travel? Explain your answer.

_____

_____

_____

_____

_____

_____

_____

_____

_____

_____

_____

_____

_____

_____

49. With so many suppliers' websites accessible to consumers for direct booking, how can an enterprising travel agent succeed in the industry?

_____

_____

_____

_____

_____

_____

_____

_____

_____

_____

_____

_____

_____

8-8

How to Start a
Home Based
Travel Agency
Workbook

Notes

Module Nine
Travel
Resources,
Reference
Materials
and Files

Module Nine
Travel Resources,
Reference Materials
and Files

Workbook Exercises 50-53

To Accompany
Second-half of Chapter 13
& Chapter 14

By completing this module you will:

• Identify and select the resources, reference materials and related supplier goods that you will need for your business to succeed.

• Arrange the materials/information into an organized filing system.

• Integrate an effective filing system into your business operation.

9-2

How to Start a
Home Based
Travel Agency
Workbook

Notes

50. The TravelProfessionalNetwork.com has been identified as an excellent on-line resource. Identify two (2) reasons a home-based travel entrepreneur would find this resource of value.

_____

_____

_____

_____

_____

_____

_____

_____

_____

_____

_____

_____

_____

_____

_____

51. Why is the task of building travel bookmarks important?

_____

_____

_____

_____

_____

_____

_____

_____

_____

_____

_____

_____

9-3

**Module Nine
Travel
Resources,
Reference
Materials
and Files**

9-4

How to Start a Home Based Travel Agency Workbook

Notes

52. Let's assume that you plan to specialize in selling cruises and are in the process of organizing your bookmark files. Outline a logical hierarchal format in which to arrange these files.

_____
_____
_____
_____
_____
_____
_____
_____
_____
_____
_____
_____
_____
_____
_____
_____
_____
_____
_____
_____
_____
_____
_____
_____
_____
_____
_____
_____
_____
_____
_____

9-5

**Module Nine
Travel
Resources,
Reference
Materials
and Files**

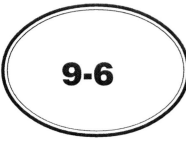

9-6

How to Start a Home Based Travel Agency Workbook

Notes

53. The previous question was hypothetical. Now let's deal in reality. Think about your business plan and the specific aspects of travel that will be your primary focus. Outline a logical hierarchal format for arranging your bookmarks.

_____

_____

_____

_____

_____

_____

_____

_____

_____

_____

_____

_____

_____

_____

_____

_____

_____

_____

_____

_____

_____

_____

_____

_____

_____

_____

_____

9-7

**Module Nine
Travel
Resources,
Reference
Materials
and Files**

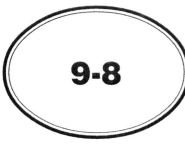

9-8

**How to Start a
Home Based
Travel Agency
Workbook**

Notes

Module Ten
Developing a
Marketing Plan

Workbook Exercises 54-58

**To Accompany
Text Chapter 15**

By completing this module you will:

• *Define your target market.*

• *Discover the most positive and cost-effective means for you to establish market exposure.*

• *Apply this knowledge to determine your marketing budget and allocate funds accordingly.*

• *Prepare a basic marketing plan for your first year of operation*

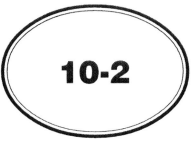

10-2

How to Start a Home Based Travel Agency Workbook

Notes

54. What is a marketing plan?

_____
_____
_____
_____
_____
_____
_____
_____
_____
_____
_____
_____
_____
_____

55. Why is a marketing plan so important to the success of your business?

_____
_____
_____
_____
_____
_____
_____
_____
_____
_____
_____
_____
_____
_____
_____
_____

10-4

How to Start a Home Based Travel Agency Workbook

Notes

56. It is time to take some action again. First, what resources do you plan to use in defining your market? Now, take some time to explore those resources, before going on to the next question.

_____
_____
_____
_____
_____
_____
_____
_____
_____
_____
_____
_____
_____
_____

57. When you developed your business plan you were asked to identify the market you intended to pursue. Armed with the research you have just completed, has your focus changed? Once again, identify your target market.

_____
_____
_____
_____
_____
_____
_____
_____
_____
_____
_____
_____
_____
_____

10-6

How to Start a Home Based Travel Agency Workbook

Notes

58. Now, consider your target market and develop your marketing plan.

a). How much money are you planning to allocate for marketing the first year?

_____

_____

_____

b). What marketing techniques do you plan to use consistently?

_____

_____

_____

_____

_____

c). Prioritize the elements in your marketing plan and allocate the funds you have budgeted proportionately amongst each component (At this point this may only be an estimate, but it will help you maintain focus).

_____

_____

_____

_____

_____

_____

_____

_____

_____

_____

_____

_____

d). Finally, map out your marketing plan on a calendar. Complete the plan for at least the first 6 months and make longer projections, if possible.

_____

_____

_____

_____

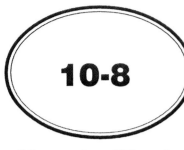

10-8

How to Start a
Home Based
Travel Agency
Workbook

Notes

Module Eleven
Communicating
With Clients

Workbook Exercises 59 - 63

**To Accompany
Text Chapters 16 & 17**

By completing this module you will:

•*Understand the value of consistency, content and appearance of newsletters.*

•*Demonstrate this knowledge by designing a prototype of your newsletter.*

•*Examine the viable sources for developing your direct mailing customer base and then formulate a potential list.*

•*Create a direct mail campaign designed to maintain contact with your existing client base while enticing potential new clients.*

11-2

How to Start a
Home Based
Travel Agency
Workbook

Notes

59. When utilizing newsletters in your marketing plan, why is it important to be consistent?

_____
_____
_____
_____
_____
_____
_____
_____
_____
_____
_____
_____
_____
_____
_____

60. Think about the very first newsletter you plan to dissemi-nate as a travel agent. List four (4) articles or information you will definitely include.

_____
_____
_____
_____
_____
_____
_____
_____
_____
_____
_____
_____
_____
_____
_____

11-4

How to Start a
Home Based
Travel Agency
Workbook

Notes

61. When you complete your newsletter, you will need to determine to whom it will be distributed. At this point, do some brainstorming and identify what sources you will use to develop your mailing list.

_____
_____
_____
_____
_____
_____
_____
_____
_____
_____
_____
_____
_____
_____

62. Now, consider one of the sources you have identified and begin to compile an actual list of names.

_____
_____
_____
_____
_____
_____
_____
_____
_____
_____
_____
_____
_____
_____
_____

11-6

How to Start a Home Based Travel Agency Workbook

Notes

_____
_____
_____
_____
_____
_____
_____
_____
_____
_____
_____
_____
_____
_____
_____
_____
_____
_____
_____
_____
_____
_____
_____
_____
_____
_____
_____
_____
_____
_____
_____
_____
_____
_____
_____
_____
_____

63. Newsletters are not the only method of communication. Think "outside the box" and develop a unique direct mail campaign that is clever or interesting.

11-8

How to Start a Home Based Travel Agency Workbook

Notes

Module Twelve
Developing an
Advertising Campaign

Workbook Exercises 64 - 68

To Accompany
Text Chapters 18 & 19

By completing this module you will:

• *Examine the various advertising and promotional opportunities available to grow your business.*

• *Determine the most cost-effective, productive advertising and promotional venue(s) to accomplish your marketing goals.*

• *Design a promotional campaign to gain maximum exposure in your community.*

12-2

How to Start a
Home Based
Travel Agency
Workbook

Notes

64. Implementing a viable advertising campaign is a challenge, state one of the issues that make this such a difficult task.

_____

_____

_____

_____

_____

_____

_____

_____

_____

_____

_____

_____

65. Determined to overcome the obstacles of establishing a successful advertising campaign, select one advertising opportunity you plan to explore and detail your plan of action.

_____

_____

_____

_____

_____

_____

_____

_____

_____

_____

_____

_____

_____

12-3

**Module Twelve
Develoing an
Advertising
Campaign**

12-4

How to Start a Home Based Travel Agency Workbook

Notes

66. From the list of travel promotions mentioned in Chapter 19, which ones do you find most appealing and viable for your business focus?

_____
_____
_____
_____
_____
_____
_____
_____
_____
_____
_____
_____
_____

67. Select one of these promotional ideas (or create one of your own) and develop a plan for implementation.

_____
_____
_____
_____
_____
_____
_____
_____
_____
_____
_____
_____
_____
_____
_____

12-6

How to Start a Home Based Travel Agency Workbook

Notes

68. Some suggestions were made for places to gain exposure to new potential clients. Thinking about your own situation, make a list of the most feasible opportunities for making contacts in your community.

_____
_____
_____
_____
_____
_____
_____
_____
_____
_____
_____
_____
_____
_____
_____
_____
_____
_____
_____
_____
_____
_____
_____
_____
_____
_____

12-8

How to Start a Home Based Travel Agency Workbook

Notes

13-1

Module
Thirteen
New Travel
Marketing
Techniques

Module Thirteen New Travel Marketing Techniques

Workbook Exercises 69 -74

To Accompany
Text Chapters 20 & 21

By completing this module you will:

• *Recognize the travel marketing opportunities the technological revolution has made available.*

• *Understand database marketing and how it can be utilized to your best advantage.*

• *Develop a plan to implement one or more of these direct sales techniques into your marketing program.*

13-2

How to Start a
Home Based
Travel Agency
Workbook

Notes

69. Cold calls, canvassing and telemarketing are all ways to grow your business. Describe how you would use one these direct sales techniques to execute a program to gain clients.

_____
_____
_____
_____
_____
_____
_____
_____
_____
_____
_____
_____
_____
_____

70. When meeting travelers while traveling, there is one major ethical issue that travel agents must be cognizant. What is that very important rule to remember?

_____
_____
_____
_____
_____
_____
_____
_____
_____
_____
_____
_____
_____
_____
_____
_____

13-4

How to Start a
Home Based
Travel Agency
Workbook

Notes

71. The technological revolution has created a number of new travel marketing opportunities. Compile a list of those you think will be advantageous for growing your business.

_____
_____
_____
_____
_____
_____
_____
_____
_____
_____
_____
_____
_____

72. Networking is critical to your success. How do you define "networking"?

_____
_____
_____
_____
_____
_____
_____
_____
_____
_____
_____
_____
_____
_____

13-5

Module
Thirteen
New Travel
Marketing
Techniques

13-6

How to Start a
Home Based
Travel Agency
Workbook

Notes

73. What is database marketing?

_____

_____

_____

_____

_____

_____

_____

_____

_____

_____

_____

_____

_____

74. Identify three (3) of the benefits of utilizing a Contact Management software program?

_____

_____

_____

_____

_____

_____

_____

_____

_____

_____

_____

_____

_____

_____

_____

13-7

**Module
Thirteen
New Travel
Marketing
Techniques**

13-8

How to Start a Home Based Travel Agency Workbook

Notes

14-1

Module
Fourteen
The Internet:
Establishing
Your Web
Presence

Module Fourteen
The Internet: Establishing
Your Web Presence

Workbook Exercises 75 - 81

To Accompany
Text Chapter 22

By completing this module you will:

• *Explore the various types of websites you may choose to develop.*

• *Define your website objective(s).*

• *Develop your websites content and functionality.*

• *Implement a plan to build and market your website.*

14-2

How to Start a Home Based Travel Agency Workbook

Notes

75. In developing your website presence there are a number of types of websites you can create. What type or types do you plan to develop?

_____
_____
_____
_____
_____
_____
_____
_____
_____
_____
_____
_____
_____
_____
_____

76. In terms of profitability, state the objective of your web.

_____
_____
_____
_____
_____
_____
_____
_____
_____
_____
_____
_____
_____
_____
_____
_____
_____
_____

14-4

**How to Start a
Home Based
Travel Agency
Workbook**

Notes

77. What is a "domain name" and why is it valuable to the success of your website?

_____

_____

_____

_____

_____

_____

_____

_____

_____

_____

_____

_____

_____

78. As you plan your website's presence, based on its purpose, brainstorm and compile a list of 10 possible "keyword domain names" that might be important in your business. (Remember: think about the relevance to a client's Internet search for information that will direct them to your site.)

_____

_____

_____

_____

_____

_____

_____

_____

_____

_____

_____

_____

_____

_____

Module Fourteen The Internet: Establishing Your Web Presence

14-6

How to Start a Home Based Travel Agency Workbook

Notes

79. Once you are ready to launch your website, identify the two things you will need to "go live" on the Internet?

_____

_____

_____

_____

_____

_____

_____

_____

_____

_____

_____

_____

_____

_____

80. There are many different opportunities for marketing your website. Name four (4) of them.

_____

_____

_____

_____

_____

_____

_____

_____

_____

_____

_____

_____

_____

_____

_____

_____

14-7

**Module
Fourteen
The Internet:
Establishing
Your Web
Presence**

14-8

How to Start a Home Based Travel Agency Workbook

Notes

81. Select one of these marketing techniques that you are most comfortable using and explain how you plan to pursue its implementation.

**Module
Fourteen
The Internet:
Establishing
Your Web
Presence**

14-10

How to Start a Home Based Travel Agency Workbook

Notes

Module Fifteen
Organizing Your
Marketing Files

Workbook Exercises 82 - 84

**To Accompany
Text Chapter 23**

By completing this module you will:

•*Differentiate between the information gathered on a Client Profile Form and a Client Questionnaire and Market Survey.*

•*Arrange the client data you collect to effectively manage your clients.*

•*Use these tools to integrate a proactive marketing campaign designed to maintain maximum client contact.*

15-2

How to Start a Home Based Travel Agency Workbook

Notes

82. What is the difference between a Passenger Profile Form and Client Questionnaire and Market Survey?

_____
_____
_____
_____
_____
_____
_____
_____
_____
_____
_____
_____
_____

83. Why are both documents important to the success of your business?

_____
_____
_____
_____
_____
_____
_____
_____
_____
_____
_____
_____
_____
_____
_____
_____
_____

15-4

How to Start a
Home Based
Travel Agency
Workbook

Notes

84. As the name implies, a Client Action Card is your call to action. Think about how you might want to organize this file and delineate the parameters you plan to use.

_____

_____

_____

_____

_____

_____

_____

_____

_____

_____

_____

_____

_____

_____

_____

_____

_____

_____

_____

_____

_____

_____

_____

_____

_____

_____

_____

_____

_____

15-5

**Module Fifteen
Organizing
Your Marketing
Files**

15-6

How to Start a
Home Based
Travel Agency
Workbook

Notes

Module Sixteen
Legal Aspects of
The Travel Industry

Workbook Exercises 85 - 94

**To Accompany
Text Chapter 25**

By completing this module you will:

•*Recognize the legal issues you will encounter as a travel professional.*

•*Discover the legalities of establishing and operating a travel business in your city/state.*

•*Modify your business plan to encompass your legal responsibilities.*

•*Evaluate your business practices and organizational procedures to assure compliance with all requisite travel laws.*

16-2

How to Start a Home Based Travel Agency Workbook

Notes

85. Legal issues are a reality of any business endeavor. What is Errors and Omissions insurance, and why is it so important?

_____

_____

_____

_____

_____

_____

_____

_____

_____

_____

_____

_____

_____

86. How might a limited power of attorney help you with a client credit card dispute?

_____

_____

_____

_____

_____

_____

_____

_____

_____

_____

_____

_____

_____

_____

16-3

**Module Sixteen
Legal Aspects
of the Travel
Industry**

16-4

How to Start a Home Based Travel Agency Workbook

Notes

_____
_____
_____
_____
_____
_____
_____
_____
_____
_____
_____
_____
_____
_____
_____
_____
_____
_____
_____
_____
_____
_____
_____
_____
_____
_____
_____
_____
_____
_____
_____
_____
_____
_____

87. What is a Universal Credit Card Charge Form (UCCF) and what information is required? Why is it important?

_____

_____

_____

_____

_____

_____

_____

_____

_____

_____

_____

_____

_____

_____

88. One of the most important jobs a travel agent has is to research each detail of a transaction and disclose their findings to the client. Why is it important for you to make sure your disclosures are in writing?

_____

_____

_____

_____

_____

_____

_____

_____

_____

_____

_____

_____

_____

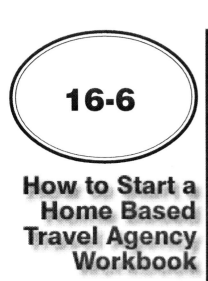

16-6

How to Start a Home Based Travel Agency Workbook

Notes

89. What is "Agency Disclosure" and why is it important to you?

_____

_____

_____

_____

_____

_____

_____

_____

_____

_____

_____

_____

_____

_____

90. Compile a list of specific items that should be disclosed to clients.

_____

_____

_____

_____

_____

_____

_____

_____

_____

_____

_____

_____

_____

_____

_____

_____

16-7

**Module Sixteen
Legal Aspects
of the Travel
Industry**

16-8

How to Start a
Home Based
Travel Agency
Workbook

Notes

91. What are the requirements for filing a Fictitious Business Name statement in your state?

_____
_____
_____
_____
_____
_____
_____
_____
_____
_____
_____
_____
_____
_____

92. What are the specific requirements for obtaining a business license in your city and state?

City: _____

_____
_____
_____
_____
_____

State: _____

_____
_____
_____
_____
_____
_____

16-9

**Module Sixteen
Legal Aspects
of the Travel
Industry**

16-10

How to Start a
Home Based
Travel Agency
Workbook

Notes

93. Some states have Seller of Travel Laws. What is your state's requirement?

_____
_____
_____
_____
_____

94. There are ethical and legal issues travel agents must consider as they sell travel in our highly mobile and transient society. In a hypothetical situation, let's assume you live in Ohio and sell cruises to clients who live in another state. What are your obligations, as it relates to Seller of Travel Laws?

California: _____

_____
_____
_____
_____
_____

Florida: _____

_____
_____
_____
_____
_____

Nevada: _____

_____
_____
_____
_____

Oter states in which you might conduct business: _____

_____
_____
_____
_____
_____

16-12

How to Start a Home Based Travel Agency Workbook

Notes

17-1

Module
Seventeen
Travel Agent
Issues:
Education,
Professionalism,
Tax and Travel
Benefits

Module Seventeen Travel Agent Issues: Education, Professionalism, and Tax and Travel Benefits

Workbook Exercises 95 - 100

To Accompany
Text Chapters 24, 26, 27 & 28

By completing this module you will:

• *Analyze your educational needs in order to become a successful travel entrepreneur.*

• *Establish the means by which you plan to develop and maintain your professionalism.*

• *Predict the travel benefits you anticipate receiving.*

• *Determine the tax benefits for which you qualify.*

17-2

How to Start a
Home Based
Travel Agency
Workbook

Notes

95. What kind of travel benefits are you expecting to gain as a travel agent? How do plan to acquire them?

_____
_____
_____
_____
_____
_____
_____
_____
_____
_____
_____
_____
_____
_____

96. As a home-based travel entrepreneur, what kind of tax benefits are you anticipating?

_____
_____
_____
_____
_____
_____
_____
_____
_____
_____
_____
_____
_____
_____
_____
_____

17-3

Module Seventeen Travel Agent Issues: Education, Professionalism, Tax and Travel Benefits

17-4

How to Start a Home Based Travel Agency Workbook

Notes

97. If you plan to use your home office as a tax deduction, what criteria will need to be met to qualify?

_____
_____
_____
_____
_____
_____
_____
_____
_____
_____
_____
_____
_____
_____
_____
_____
_____
_____
_____

98. All business travel and entertainment expenses are not totally tax deductible. Name three (3) cases where a deduction would not be allowed and three (3) examples of allowable expenses.

Not Allowed: _____
_____
_____
_____
_____

Allowed: _____
_____
_____
_____
_____
_____
_____
_____

17-6

How to Start a
Home Based
Travel Agency
Workbook

Notes

99. By now you should have a good perspective on how you will develop and implement your entrepreneurial dreams as a travel professional. What means do you plan to pursue to develop your knowledge of the travel industry? Create a timetable for your educational pursuits and skill development.

_____

_____

_____

_____

_____

_____

_____

_____

_____

_____

_____

_____

_____

100. In addition to an ongoing plan to pursue educational opportunities, you should have an idea of how you plan to stay connected with the travel industry at large. Summarize the methods you will employ to maintain your professionalism.

_____

_____

_____

_____

_____

_____

_____

_____

_____

_____

_____

_____

_____

Module Seventeen Travel Agent Issues: Education, Professionalism, Tax and Travel Benefits

17-8

**How to Start a
Home Based
Travel Agency
Workbook**

Notes

A Checklist
For Getting Started

To help you get started on your venture (and to establish a starting budget), the following is a breakdown of activities so that you can establish the appropriate budget allocation to get going. Where you do not know the amount of money that may be required you can simply "guesstimate" the information for the purpose of establishing a budget.

Developing this information before you start your project is important, and it will help you to decide the viability of your business concept. Spend as much time as necessary to establish this road map, as the more time you spend on this effort the faster and more efficiently you will progress towards the reality of starting your own home-based travel business.

Remember to be as honest, as possible when determining the amounts that you are going to budget and the priority of the item budgeted. Place priorities on those items that are going to enhance your success rather than on areas that may do little to propel you into your business. Accessing the many benefits of HBTANetwork.com, as an example, will allow you to leap frog over many hurdles that new entrepreneurs face when starting up their business. By taking advantage of agent networks such as HomeBasedTravelAgent.com and accessing the HBTACommunity.com you will move forward faster than you can imagine. Certainly you should invest in technology at the start of your business and in the knowledge of how to best exploit the technology as well.

CL-2

How to Start a
Home Based
Travel Agency
Workbook

Notes

_____
_____
_____
_____
_____
_____
_____
_____
_____
_____
_____
_____
_____
_____
_____
_____
_____
_____
_____
_____
_____
_____
_____
_____
_____
_____
_____
_____
_____
_____
_____
_____
_____
_____
_____
_____

Planning Activity

Every business should start with a well thought out concept and plan before the first dime is spent. Without this roadmap it is very difficult to engage in a meaningful venture.

Develop a Business Concept
Develop a Business Plan
Develop a Marketing Plan

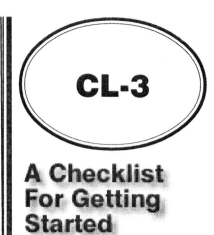

CL-3

A Checklist For Getting Started

Organizational Activity

Setting up the business: These first steps are necessary to establish yourself in the travel industry.

File a Fictitious Business Name Statement _____
Obtain local business license _____
Open bank account(s) _____
Obtain Seller of Travel bond or Restitution Fund _____
(Check state requirements)

Register with state as Seller of Travel _____
(Check state requirements)

Design and print stationery _____
    Letterhead _____
    Envelopes _____
    Business cards _____
    Brochure _____
    Other _____

Total Organizational Costs _____

Start Up Activity

Furnishing your home office: While you may be tempted to use the kitchen table as your base until you get going, an investment in quality office furniture will yield huge dividends in productivity.

    Desk _____
    Office Chair _____
    Lighting _____
    File Cabinet _____
    Book Cases _____
    Telephone (s) _____
    Office Chair Pads_____

CL-4

How to Start a Home Based Travel Agency Workbook

Notes

Wall Treatments_____
Stapler, Calculator, Misc. Items_____
Supplies _____

Equipping your home office: You probably already have a personal computer and telephone that would suffice until your business expands to a point where you need to upgrade. You should, however, factor in any cost you are likely to incur the first year.

Personal Computer _____
Printer _____
Software _____
Office Suite _____
Publishing _____
Facsimile Management _____
HTML Editor_____
Photo Editor_____
Facsimile Machine _____
Web Site_____

Joining Industry Associations and Begining Your Educational Program(s): You will certainly want to join one of the travel industry associations. In addition that are several other groups you might ant to investigate.

ARC VTC_____
CLIA _____
Other _____

Setting up your reference library: You will need the trade publications to really get started and stay current in your business. The rest may not be the most important place to spend money unless you are specializing and need detailed information.

Trade Publications_____
Hotel Books _____
Travel Magazines _____
Travel Agent Websites
    HBTANetwork.com.com _____
    HomeBasedTravelAgent.com _____
    HBTACommunity.com_____
    Other_____
    Other _____

Total Start-Up Costs _____

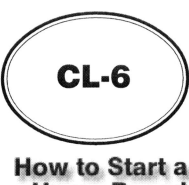

CL-6

**How to Start a
Home Based
Travel Agency
Workbook**

Notes

Supplier Activity

Making initial contract and securing working relationship with suppliers is a key chore to establishing your business. One person may simply work with a local agency requiring no investment, while others may elect to join IC Networks and consortia and invest thousands.

Your Host Agency _____
Consortia _____
Miscellaneous Suppliers _____

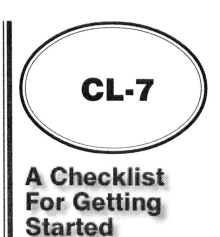

CL-7

A Checklist For Getting Started

Establishing Your Monthly Operating Budget

One of the most important tasks you should undertake before launching your new business is to determine the average monthly cash flow needed to maintain your business. Following are some of the more common monthly expenses you will experience. By understanding the nature of your overhead it will help you adjust your activity for maximum productivity.

Advertising
    Yellow Pages _____
    Newspaper _____
    Newsletters _____
    Advertising Specialties _____
    Other _____
Automated Reservations System
    User's Fees _____
    On-Line Services Fees _____
Bank Charges
    Checking Account _____
    Trust Account _____
    Interest on Loans _____
Dues
    Association _____
    CLIA or ARC VTC _____
    Other _____
Equipment Rental
    Office Equipment _____
    Postage Equipment _____
    Other _____
Insurance
    Business Liability _____
    E & O Insurance _____

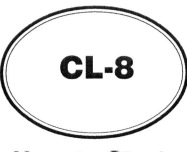

CL-8

How to Start a Home Based Travel Agency Workbook

Notes

Postage and Delivery
    Postage _____
    Bulk Mail _____
    Delivery Charges _____
    Other _____
Printing
    Stationery _____
    Business Cards _____
    Brochure _____
    Newsletters _____
    Other _____
Professional Fees
    Consultant _____
    Attorney _____
    Accountant _____
Subscriptions
    Hotel & Travel Index _____
    Trade Publications
        Agenjt @ Home _____
        Recommend Magazine _____
        Travel Weekly _____
        Travel Agent Magazine _____
        TravelAge West _____
        Other _____
    Other _____
    Other _____
Telephone & Communications
    Business Lines _____
    Facsimile Lines _____
    Long Distance Usage _____
    Local Usage _____
    Other _____
Travel
    Sales Calls _____
    Inspection Tours _____
    Ticket Delivery_____
    Fam/Cruise/Seminars _____
Utilities
    Electricity _____
    Gas _____
    Other _____
Miscellaneous Expenses _____

Total Monthly Expenses _____

CL-9

A Checklist For Getting Started

CL-10

How to Start a Home Based Travel Agency Workbook

Notes

How to Start a
Home Based Travel Agency
Test

Congratulations! By now, you have probably finished reading the study course, completed the workbook and checklist for getting started and are about ready to get going on your own travel business. Here is a test that you can take to see how much of the information you have absorbed. If you find yourself unsure of the answers to some of the questions, find the section in the text that deals with the topic of the question and find answer. This test is designed to test the depth of your understanding of the material.

I hope you enjoyed the study course and workbook and that it has helped you along your way to becoming a successful travel entrepreneur. The travel industry is a wonderful and vibrant business, and I am sure you will find everything that you are looking for in your own home-based travel agency.

Be sure to visit www.HomeBasedTravelAgent.com to review other books written by Tom and Joanie Ogg CTC, MCC that will help you along the way. Also, don't forget to visit www.HBTACommunity.com and join this vibrant social network for home based travel professionals. Now that you are under way, you qualify to join. It is FUN and it is FREE!

Tom Ogg

Test-2

How to Start a
Home Based
Travel Agency
Workbook

How to Start a Home Based Travel Agency Test

1. The reason for the increasing number of home-based travel agents is:
    A. Technology
    B. The elimination of airline commissions
    C. An entrepreneurial environment
    D. All of the above
    E. B and C only

2. A home-based agent may be:
    A. An employee
    B. An independent contractor
    C. A business owner
    D. All of the above
    E. B & C

3. As an independent contractor, a home-based travel agent should have at least two types of insurance, they are:
    A. Credit card insurance and errors and omissions insurance
    B. Life insurance and homeowners insurance
    C. Errors and omissions insurance and home owners insurance
    D. Credit card insurance and home owners insurance
    E. Errors and omissions insurance and life insurance

4. At the end of the year, host agencies and suppliers report an independent contractor's earnings on an IRS form:
    A. W-2
    B. Schedule C
    C. 1099
    D. 2047
    E. 1040

5. Which of the following criteria would the IRS use to determine if one was either an employee or an independent contractor?
    A. Control of the agency over the individual
    B. Existence of a written contract or Agreement
    C. Who provides the tools of the trade
    D. How earnings are reported
    E. Risk of profit or loss
    F. All of the above

Test-4

**How to Start a
Home Based
Travel Agency
Workbook**

6. The most ethical way to hold clients' funds is in:
    A. Your personal bank account
    B. Your business checking account
    C. Your business trust account
    D. A home safe

7. As an I.C. "Tools of the trade" are generally provided by:
    A. The suppliers
    B. The independent contractor
    C. The host agency
    D. All of the above
    E. None of the above

8. CRS refers to:
    A. Complete Reference Service
    B. Computerized Reservations System
    C. Client Reference System
    D. Computer Referral System
    E. None of the above

9. A host agency / independent contractor agreement must:
    A. Be for a specific period of time
    B. Include an independent contractor statement
    C. Identify the parties to the agreement
    D. All of the Above
    E. A and C only

10. What does TSI stand for?
    A. Travel Service Intermediary
    B. Travel Service Identification
    C. Travel Security Information
    D. Travel Supplier Information
    E. None of the above

11. Ways to increase profitability include:
    A. Increase yields
    B. Decrease costs
    C. Increase productivity
    D. B and C only
    E. All of the above

12. Which of the following items are necessary to disclose to a client?
    A. Agency relationship
    B. The offer and acceptance or rejection of travel insurance
    C. Your cancellation and change policies and the supplier's.
    D. A and C only
    E. All of the above

Test-5

How to Start a Home Based Travel Agency Test

Test-6

How to Start a Home Based Travel Agency Workbook

13. Some of the most important benefits of travel insurance are:
    A. Medical evacuation
    B. Trip cancellation/interruption damages
    C. Medical and emergency coverage
    D. A and B only
    E. All of the above

14. An agency relationship is considered to be a:
    A. A promise to perform
    B. A fiduciary relationship
    C. The highest possible standard of performance in business
    D. A and B only
    E. All of the above

15. Monies paid to an independent contractor by a client become the independent contractors:
    A. When paid to the independent contractor by the client
    B. When the check is cashed
    C. When it is deposited into the I.C.s bank account
    D. When it is deposited into the I.C.'s trust account
    E. Never

16. If an agent sells less than $100,000 per year, which of the following is not required:
    A. A local business license
    B. Register as a seller of travel in their state
    C. Comply with all zoning laws
    D. B and C only
    E. None of the above

17. Payment to suppliers using the client's credit card:
    A. is illegal
    B. Affords the client additional protection against the financial failure of the supplier
    C. Slows payment of the commission
    D. B and C only
    E. None of the above

18. What does FIT stand for?
    A. Foreign or Free Independent Travel
    B. Free International Transfer
    C. Foreign Immigration Transportation
    D. What an I.C. has when a client makes too many changes
    E. None of the above

Test-7

How to Start a Home Based Travel Agency Test

Test-8

How to Start a
Home Based
Travel Agency
Workbook

19. Which of these items are important for projecting a strong professional image?
  A. Maintaining a separate business telephone line
  B. Operating with a Federal Taxpayer ID Number
  C. Using top quality paper for business cards and stationery
  D. A and C only
  E. All of the above

20. What should be your first consideration when developing a business plan?
  A. Find ways to fund your business start-up
  B. Project your income and expenses
  C. Define your expectations
  D. Establish your business name
  E. None of the above

21. The purpose of developing a marketing plan is:
  A. To retain existing clients
  B. Develop new clients
  C. Prospect for potential clients
  D. B and C only
  E. All of the above

22. The keys to a successful direct mail campaign/newsletter are:
  A. Inclusion of a call to action by the recipient
  B. Consistency
  C. Limiting content to focus on one specific topic
  D. A and B only
  E. All of the above

23. In defining your website objective(s) you should consider:
  A. Profitability
  B. The type of website you wish to create
  C. How much time and resources you plan to commit
  D. A, B, and C
  E. B and C only

24. Which of the following is not necessary for a UCCF (Universal Credit Card Charge Form) to be fully compliant?
  A. Original signature of cardholder
  B. Valid authorization code from credit card company
  C. Copy of card holder's drivers license or passport
  D. Imprint of front of credit card
  E. Imprint of back of credit card

Test-9

How to Start a Home Based Travel Agency Test

Test-10

How to Start a Home Based Travel Agency Workbook

25. When establishing a home-based travel agency the legal way to organize the business is:
    A. As a sole proprietorship
    B. As a partnership
    C. As a corporation
    D. A and B only
    E. All of the above

26. Currently a travel agent license is required in all states:
    True
    False

27. True independent contractors are free to do business with anyone they want:
    True
    False

28. A host agency demanding exclusivity may be violating the independent contractor classification with the IRS:
    True
    False

29. An independent contractor is free to use money paid by clients for deposits and final payments, as they see fit until the supplier demands it:
    True
    False

30. www.Checkacode.com verifies IATAN registrants:
    True
    False

31. An independent contractor doing business as a separate legal entity has primary liability for their actions:
    True
    False

32. Disclosure to consumers of an independent contractor's agency relationship is not necessary:
    True
    False

33. Travel agent/client disclosure is best done in writing bearing the client's signature agreeing with the disclosure:
    True
    False

Test-11

How to Start a Home Based Travel Agency Test

Test-12

**How to Start a
Home Based
Travel Agency
Workbook**

34. Agency is established by mutual agreement:
    True
    False

35. A written agreement between an independent contractor and a host agency is optional:
    True
    False

36. An outside sales agent can be a job description for either an independent contractor or an employee:
    True
    False

37. It is illegal to charge clients service fees for selling airline tickets.
    True
    False

38. Errors and omissions and general liability insurance is recommended for independent contractors:
    True
    False

39. An independent travel agent may have more than 1 host agency:
    True
    False

40. Travel agents must obtain a federal travel agent license before they can sell travel:
    True
    False

41. It is OK to use clients' payments for your own personal use, as long as the payments to the suppliers are made on time:
    True
    False

42. A travel agent must register in every state in which they have clients residing, if the state has a travel agent registration program:
    True
    False

43. Being able to solicit passengers for their business is just one of the many benefits of traveling on a travel agent's rate while on a cruise:
    True
    False

Test-13

How to Start a Home Based Travel Agency Test

Test-14

How to Start a Home Based Travel Agency Workbook

44. ATPEW x (YPT-CPT) is the formula used to determine travel agency profitability:
    True
    False

45. A Client Security Trust Account should only be used when booking large groups:
    True
    False

46. When establishing your business name, you must register with the Federal government, in addition to complying with state requirements:
    True
    False

47. In order to work with suppliers, a home-based travel agent must have an IATAN, CLIA or ARC identification number:
    True
    False

48. A key word domain name is critical to establishing a significant web presence:
    True
    False

49. All of your business travel and entertainment expenses are tax deductible:
    True
    False

50. Contact management software is a database which allows you to control the flow of communication between you and your client:
    True
    False

Test-16

How to Start a Home Based Travel Agency Workbook